Are They Alike?

How growing up and growing older can be fun and funny

MW01079125

Story by
J. Michael McIntyre

Illustration by
Ann Thomas

Copyright © 2021 J. Michael McIntyre
Published by J. Michael McIntyre, Mequon, WI
ISBN 978-0-578-84316-2
First printed edition 2021
All rights reserved

No parts of this book may be reproduced in any
form or by any electronic or mechanical means,
including information storage and retrieval systems,
without written permission from the author, except
for the use of brief quotations in a book review.

Story by J. Michael McIntyre
Illustration by Ann Thomas
Design by J. Michael McIntyre

Visit **www.aretheyalike.com** for
information about *Are They Alike?*, Ann
and Mike, the inside scoop and freebies.

Please contact the author at:
author@aretheyalike.com

**Please
Write A
Review**

**Authors love to
hear from their
readers!** Please let
Mike McIntyre know
what you thought about
Are They Alike? By leaving a
review on Amazon or your preferred
online store, it will help parents, children
and grandparents find the book. (If you are
under 13, please ask a grown-up to help). Thank You!

Many Hands

No creative endeavor is the product of a single individual. I am grateful to all who generously offered encouragement, suggestions and critical eyes. A special thanks to my mother who introduced me to great books even when I balked at reading; to my wife, Carol, whose love of children's books is infectious; to Ann Thomas for taking this journey; and to our grandchildren who keep me young and laughing.

I'm Bree's big sister, Emma.

We live in Arborville.

Our Grandpa lives next door.

I think Grandpa and Bree are alike.

Grandpa doesn't.

He says he's old and Bree's young.

And he's a man and she's a girl.

Come with me. Let's see!

Drops

Bald

Sprinkle

Grandpa helps care for Bree.

Bree is bald like Grandpa.

"I like my bald head because I know when

it starts sprinkling," says Grandpa.

Bree's new walker helps her first steps.

Grandpa's walker helps his new knee.

Our dog, Trixie, doesn't like walkers.

Plops

Tops

Squirts

Bree's bib keeps drops off her tops.

Grandpa's napkin keeps squirts

off his shirts.

Are they alike, Grandpa and Bree?

Keep on reading and you will see!

"My fingers are stiff. It's hard to

tie my shoes," says Grandpa.

Bree tries to tie her shoes, but the laces tangle.

Grandpa takes Bree to Sal's Shoe Shop.

Their new sneakers have sticky straps.

Ready
Set
Go!

Grandpa and Bree like

to race their trikes.

"Emma, yell go!" says Bree.

Three wheels keep them from

going head over heels.

Go Pruners Go!

We like to go to Arborville's high school basketball games. "Go Pruners go!" we yell. Bree gets in free because she's little. Grandpa gets in free because he's a grandpa.

Are they alike, Grandpa and Bree?

Keep on reading and you will see!

Wiggle Wobble Gooey

Grandpa cuts corn off Bree's cob.

Then he cuts corn off his cob.

Bree's top tooth wiggles.

Grandpa's bottom tooth wobbles.

They can't eat chewy, gooey food but they

love apple juice and chocolate mousse.

Words

Books

Whisper

Every week we go to the library.

"Emma, will you help me?" asks Bree.

Grandpa and Bree choose books with big print.

"The words are easy to see," whispers Bree.

Grandpa agrees.

Bree and Grandpa eat burgers at Downtown Diner.

Bree dangles her feet and spins the stool.

Grandpa orders from the seniors menu.

Bree orders from the kids menu.

Their burgers are the perfect size.

Are they alike, Grandpa and Bree?

Keep on reading and you will see!

Jog
Ear
Hear

Bree jogs to pop music streamed in her ear.

Grandpa loves jazz, but not while jogging.

Grandpa wears an ear bud too.

It helps him hear.

Bree bags groceries at Happy Hen.

She spends her money on music.

Grandpa bags groceries with Bree on Tuesdays.

He spends his money on warm winter vacations.

Stop!

Look!

Listen

Grandpa renews his driver's license but

doesn't drive after dark.

Bree gets her driver's license but doesn't

stay out late. "Grandpa, can I drive you to

the Happy Hen?" asks Bree.

Are They Alike?

Bree is in college. She lives with friends in Magnolia Hall. Grandpa lives next door to Bree's college with friends in Ginkgo Grove.

"Bree, I love that we still go to the library every week," says Grandpa. "Me too," says Bree.

Grandpa was right. They are different.

And I was right, they are alike!

Made in the USA
Monee, IL
18 October 2021

80273951R00021